fast thinking: your own appraisal

PEARSON EDUCATION LIMITED

Head Office:
Edinburgh Gate
Harlow CM20 2JE
Tel: +44 (0)1279 623623
Fax: +44 (0)1279 431059

London Office:
128 Long Acre
London WC2E 9AN
Tel: +44 (0)20 7447 2000
Fax: +44 (0)20 7240 5771
Website: www.fast-thinking.com

First published in Great Britain in 2001

© Pearson Education Limited 2001

The right of Richard Templar to be identified as Author
of this Work has been asserted by him in accordance
with the Copyright, Designs and Patents Act 1988.

ISBN 0 273 65482 9

British Library Cataloguing in Publication Data
A CIP catalogue record for this book can be obtained from the British Library

10 9 8 7 6 5 4 3 2 1

Typeset by Pantek Arts Ltd, Maidstone, Kent
Printed and bound in Great Britain by Ashford Colour Press, Hampshire

The Publishers' policy is to use paper manufactured from sustainable forests.

fast
thinking:
your own
appraisal

 be articulate

 make your point

 impress your boss

by Richard Templar

contents

introduction

Whoa! Don't things have a habit of creeping up on you? You put the date in your diary a while back and now it's come around. Tomorrow. Your own appraisal. And what have you done? Why, absolutely nothing of course. You forgot. It happens. But now is not the time to panic. Oh, no. Now is the time to do a little serious reading and get it sorted out. You have less than 24 hours to prepare your defence. Sorry, appraisal.

There is a lot you should have done and a lot you simply haven't time for now. What we have to do is make sure you *look* as if you've done everything, and that you come out of this looking good, appearing to be effective and in superb command of your job. No small potatoes when we've only got such a limited time. But don't despair. You've got hold of the right repair manual to help you sort this out – quickly and efficiently.

This guide will remind you what documents you are going to need, how to present them, what to say and how to say it, and how to get the most and best out of your own personal appraisal. Having an appraisal isn't an opportunity to have a quick chat or mull over how your department's been doing since the last review. No. It's much more than that. It's your own private space to discuss your job, the pitfalls and disappointments, the successes and the highs.

Your appraisal is your chance to put forward new ideas about where you think you're going, what you intend doing and how you aim to achieve more and better. It's your opportunity to ask for better resources to enable you to operate more effectively, demand more positive feedback so you can manoeuvre more efficiently, request more training, broaden your experience and generally register your feelings about your work. It isn't a departmental budget review. It isn't a salary review. It isn't a bit of a chat. It is your own appraisal and so it's vitally important to get it right and get it good. Let's do it.

This book will help you as you will need:

 tips and shortcuts for getting on top of this appraisal, fast

 guidelines for participating in a successful appraisal

 speedy information about what to say and how to say it

 checklists to make sure you haven't forgotten anything

… and all presented clearly and logically. And short enough, of course, to take in quickly. You got it.

And what if you really have run out of time and your appraisal interview is pencilled in for later this morning? Or even in one hour's time? Well, we can do it – and do it good. At the back of this book you'll find a brief guide to appraisals in a *real* hurry. Now that really is thinking at the speed of life.

So take the phone off the hook, put your feet up and enjoy a cup of coffee as we race through the important essentials of fast thinking your way to smelling of roses. And now that you know you could do it in only an hour and still look pretty cool, having a whole day seems positively extravagant, doesn't it? OK. Let's start off by looking at the seven key points of being appraised successfully.

work at the speed of life

1. Before you do anything you need to identify your objective – what you intend to achieve by being appraised, i.e. what you are going to get out of this.

2. Then you'll need to consider what documents you should have received by now and what you should have done with them – getting you ready and prepared.

3. After that we'll look at how you can have some input into where and when the interview is to be held. This will enable you to be more in control and more able to swing things your way.

4. Then we need to look at how we can agree the structure and agenda of the interview – yep, its yours and you do have a say in it.

5. What are you going to say? And how are you going to say it? Chapter 5 guides you through the right responses and the right attitude to adopt, and includes a section on difficult bosses and how to handle them.

6. We'll see how to wriggle out of trouble – sorry, justify your actions – and suggest ways to improve your performance as well as ways of accepting and handling constructive criticism. Then there's the right way to request the resources to allow this to happen. And how to follow it all up afterwards of course.

7. And finally, we will look at action plans, wrapping up the interview so both you and your boss feel confident that you are in agreement, and then the follow-up – what you have to do next. We will also look at preparing for your own appraisal in an hour and in 10 minutes – that's really thinking at the speed of life.

fast thinking gambles

So, we can get you through it quickly and efficiently. If you follow the guidelines in this book you shouldn't go far wrong or end up looking like an unprepared prat; you'll actually enjoy being appraised and have a very positive contribution to make. But there are always risks when you do things as fast as we are going to.

- ▶ You probably won't have time to make sure your job description is really up to date, that it matches with what you do now as opposed to what you were originally employed to do. These things do have a way of getting overlooked in the white hot heat of business.

- ▶ You may not have time to request a change of venue or time if either is inappropriate or unsuitable – making do with a corridor in your boss's tea-break really isn't on and you do have the right to request a postponement or an alternative interview room/place.

- ▶ You are so rushed you might not have time to complete and hand in the employee preparation document which you should have been supplied with. In fact you might be so rushed you hadn't even realised you should have had one. Going into an appraisal interview with a badly completed form – or none at all – is a bad move as it doesn't give your boss a chance to see how you feel about your job in advance – and that can lead to communication problems.

 You haven't had time to go through mentally or in note form everything important that has happened to you work-wise that may be brought up – there is nothing worse than having forgotten an important thing like upsetting a prized client and then finding it brought up at appraisal time. You'll be wrong-footed and left looking unprepared and foolish. Let's make sure it doesn't happen.

Fast thinking will get you through the appraisal interview at speed and you'll end up looking pretty cool as well as getting what you want. And that's the point of the exercise. But for next time you could do with leaving yourself a little more time. Not only can you do an even better job, but you won't feel flustered, have kittens or be bad tempered because of the pressure. You'll be looking good, staying cool and working much more effectively – and all because of a little fast thinking guide you can slip in your pocket and read in the loo. Not bad at all.

1 your objective

I know you're pushed for time and have worked out your own priority list – but this bit is important. Take a few minutes to really think about your objective before you rush off and do all those other things you consider vital. After all, you wouldn't set out on a journey without knowing where you were going and what route you were taking. The same is true of any business undertaking. You need to know your final destination, your goal. So where are you going with this appraisal? What is it you want from it? And how are you going to get there? That is your objective – knowing the answers to those questions.

You may think that having an appraisal is merely something that has to be endured, something visited upon you from on high – a sort of divine retribution for being wicked in a past life. And I'm sure a lot of employees do look at appraisals in that sort of light. But not the smart ones. Not the fast thinking ones. Not you. Your appraisal isn't a bit of a chat, or a telling off for all the things you may or may not have done wrong, or even a pat on the back if you've done well. Your appraisal should be motivating, supportive, encouraging. It should be a chance for you to put right anything that you feel is wrong about your job. It should be a formal opportunity to have your strengths and weaknesses assessed and appraised.

WHAT ELSE IS AN APPRAISAL FOR?

You can also review company procedures, look at future training, discuss your development needs and consider your future prospects. All of this can take place within the framework of your appraisal. You have to decide what *you* want *your* appraisal to be – which of these things you need clarification on or would like to pursue further. And to make that decision you have to set an objective.

But hang on, I hear you say, surely I am being appraised and have to accept whatever my boss decides, whatever agenda they set? Surely I am a passive victim in all this? Yep, for a lot of team members I am sure that is exactly how they see it. But not you, oh no. Not the smart employee.

There are ways of manoeuvring this appraisal so you get out of it what you want. And to do that you have to set your objective.

You may have to make your boss realise your worth, your potential and your importance so that they approach this appraisal in the same way that you will. You may have to motivate the lazy boss, outsmart the devious and manipulate the insipid. But run this appraisal you must if you are to get something worthwhile out of it.

thinking fast

SET ASIDE TIME

To set your objective doesn't take long. But it does take a little effort. Set aside a few minutes to decide exactly what it is you want from your appraisal – more training, extra feedback, increased supervision, increased responsibility, less monitoring, appropriate back-up, improved facilities, improved resources. You have to make the decisions about what it is you want improved to enable you to work more efficiently, feel happier, more challenged and motivated. It is your right to have these things and it is up to you to set that objective. So you need to set aside a little time to plan your journey before you leave home.

THE POOR APPRAISAL

We've all been appraised in our work career. Sometimes it was done so badly we might not have even realised that was what it was. 'How are things going?' 'Fine.' 'Well, that's alright then.'

Well, that certainly isn't good enough. We need a decent appraisal to enable us to plan our future and improve our weak areas. If we are motivated enough and sufficiently on top of our job we might not need any praise (but it's always nice to have a pat on the back) as we know we have performed well. But without a proper appraisal we can't plan ahead. And

thinking smart

REMEMBER DOING APPRAISALS YOURSELF

You may be senior enough to have conducted appraisals yourself. Remember what they have been like. Remember how difficult it is when a team member contributes nothing, merely grunts when asked a question or is late, rude or uncooperative. Make it easy for your boss by speaking freely, not being defensive, by contributing and being accommodating, helpful and obliging. You will be remembered as a cooperative team member and you'll score some brownie points.

You may have to motivate the lazy boss, outsmart the devious and manipulate the insipid. But run this appraisal you must that appraisal has to be conducted properly, recorded in writing so we can refer to it later, with an action plan so we know exactly what is required of us, and it must be of sufficient depth for us to discuss our progress and how we see our work.

So let's set that objective: to get through my appraisal as quickly and easily as possible.

Nope. Not good enough. Try again. Your objective has been appraised and has been found to be wanting. I'll give you a clue. Here are a few key words you may like to include:

- ▶ **assess**
- ▶ **consider**
- ▶ **evaluate**
- ▶ **review**
- ▶ **value**

Try again? OK: to have my current work assessed and evaluated with documented feedback, and to have my future work programme reviewed and discussed.

Good. Much better. If you approach your appraisal in the right frame of mind you should emerge from it feeling:

- ▶ **cared about**
- ▶ **motivated**
- ▶ **stimulated**
- ▶ **challenged**
- ▶ **rewarded**
- ▶ **stretched.**

Good. Now let's see how we can achieve all this quickly and efficiently.

for next time

Make sure you have signalled well in advance that you expect a proper assessment and simply aren't prepared to put up with a casual chat in the staff canteen. Make it be known that you expect:

- ▶ privacy
- ▶ sufficient time to discuss everything in depth
- ▶ an up-to-date assessment of your work performance
- ▶ a written summary of the appraisal
- ▶ an action plan, which may include suggested training and the resources for doing it.

We've all been appraised in our work career. Sometimes it was done so badly we might not have even realised that was what it was

2 preparation

So your appraisal is tomorrow and you are ready. You are ready, aren't you? And what do we mean by ready? Well, there are two things you have to do to be ready:

1. **Receive instructions from your boss.**

2. **Plan what you want to say and what you want the appraisal to achieve.**

Let's deal with each one in turn but let's get a move on, time is tight.

RECEIVE INSTRUCTIONS FROM YOUR BOSS

By now you should have had various pieces of paper from your boss regarding tomorrow's appraisal. These might, and probably should, include a memo and a pre-appraisal document of some kind. The memo should include such information as:

- your name
- your job title

- the purpose of the memo – confirming your appraisal interview is going to take place, the period it covers (six months, a year) and so on

- the purpose of the appraisal – to provide feedback on your performance and to give you an opportunity to discuss your work performance and any future training or promotion needs you have

- where and when your appraisal is to take place

- roughly how long it will last – at least an hour

- who is issuing the memo – your boss's name and job title, with their signature and the date.

And you should have had this memo at least 10 days prior to the proposed day of the appraisal. This should be a formal memo of which your boss should have kept a copy – and so should you. If you haven't had this memo by now you are quite within your rights to ask for the appraisal to be postponed until you have been notified officially – you must be given the chance to prepare yourself in advance. Getting a quick e-mail from your boss saying your appraisal is in 10 minutes' time simply isn't good enough. It is unfair and very poor staff relations indeed.

THE PRE-APPRAISAL PREPARATION DOCUMENT

The other document you should have received is a pre-appraisal preparation document. This is your opportunity to record for your boss how you feel about your job and your performance. It gives them a chance to make sure that they've got the right team member and that you are both singing from the same song sheet. If you think you've performed brilliantly and your boss thinks you've performed appallingly, this document, duly completed and returned to your boss, will give them a chance to rethink their approach. They may have the wrong person or the wrong job in mind, or the wrong idea altogether. They'll have a chance to re-evaluate before the appraisal and it will stop both of you getting off on the wrong foot and making complete fools of yourselves.

The pre-appraisal preparation document typically used to be merely a list of boxes to be ticked – you know the sort of thing:

How do you consider you have carried out the main functions of your job? Please tick box.

Well ☐

Average ☐

Badly ☐

And what did this tell us? Virtually nothing. Modern thinking now gives us lots of space to fill in our own comments. The form might look something like this:

Name:

Job title:

Date and time of appraisal:

The purpose of this form is to give you an opportunity to prepare for your appraisal so that your assessment can be as productive as possible. Please fill in the boxes as fully as possible.

They'll have a chance to re-evaluate before the appraisal and it will stop both of you getting off on the wrong foot

How do you consider you have carried out the main functions of your job?

Which tasks have you performed best, and why?

Are there any areas of your job which you feel are unclear?

Do you feel the need for any extra training and, if so, what sort of training would be helpful?

What would be helpful to you to enable you to carry out your job more successfully?

Which aspects of your job interest you the most?

Which aspects interest you least?

Are there any functions of your job at which you feel you have underachieved, and why?

How do you see your future with the company?

TAKE YOUR TIME

Once you've got this document you should have had at least a day to complete it and return it prior to the appraisal. Got yours? Good. Then take your time filling it in before returning it. Make sure you keep a copy of it so you can refer to it during the appraisal and also at any time later. Now I know that time is short and you have a lot to do but it really is important to take some time to think this document through clearly and well. This is the document your boss will have in front of them to

Make sure you keep a copy of it so you can refer to it during the appraisal and also at any time later

work from along with their own impressions and interpretations. What you say on the form will be of considerable value, so don't fill in one-word answers, make it comprehensive and full. This is your opportunity to record in writing all that you feel is good about your performance and to officially request training, extra tuition, guidance, coaching and further education – all the things you may need to improve performance and take you along to the next step of your career path. *This document is important.*

The memo and the pre-appraisal preparation document (if you don't get one there is nothing wrong with preparing your own and filling it in, just don't hand it in but keep it with you) are essential bits of paper to get. They let you know your boss is doing their job properly, and reassuring and informing you. Their job is to make sure you're not intimidated by your appraisal – it isn't a school report or a court case, nor is it an interrogation or a means of frightening team members. It is an appraisal and is an opportunity to praise and to raise issues.

IT'S A TWO-WAY PROCESS

A lot of members of staff see their appraisal as something to avoid, something to dread and get through as quickly and painlessly as possible – but not the smart team member. Oh, no. You see it as a useful and essential aspect of your work. Your appraisal should be relished, enjoyed, looked forward to, anticipated with excitement. And definitely seen as something to benefit from. It is a two-way process. Not only is it your boss's chance to appraise your performance, but it is also your chance to appraise how the company and your boss are using your time and resources. This is your opportunity to put right all that may be wrong.

thinking smart

SPRINGBOARDS

Your appraisal is an opportunity to correct anything you see wrong with your job. But not your salary. That is part of a salary review, which is another thing entirely. But the appraisal review *can* be used as a useful springboard for the salary review and the smart team member (that's you by the way; you bought this book – clever move, sensible idea, brilliant strategy) will already be planning ahead: 'If I increase my performance by learning how to use the ZX35 machine, I will be entitled to more money. I can ask at my appraisal for increased training on the ZX35 and then when the pay review comes around I'll already be one step ahead ...'

PLAN WHAT YOU WANT TO SAY AND WHAT YOU WANT THE APPRAISAL TO ACHIEVE

If you are going to turn the tables and start to get maximum benefit from the appraisal interview you have to be pretty certain what it is you want. This means knowing exactly where your strengths and weaknesses lie before you ever set foot inside the interview room. What you have to do is carry out your own appraisal, on yourself, being as objective, honest and in depth as possible. This is a ruthless and difficult mission but one that you will enjoy once you see how advantageous it is. The smart team member knows that there should be no surprises at an appraisal, which means knowing exactly:

- ▶ what you have done and what you haven't
- ▶ what you've done well and what you've done badly
- ▶ where both your successes and your failures lie
- ▶ where you've gone beyond the call of duty and where you've fallen short of it
- ▶ where you've been helpful and cooperative and where you've hindered and been obstructive
- ▶ where you've contributed to the team effort and where you most certainly haven't.

Only you can know all this stuff – and your boss, of course, and chances are they won't have forgotten anything and it will be brought up at your appraisal. Better to be forewarned, forearmed and ready for anything.

TURNING THE TABLES

So once you have worked out exactly what is likely to be brought up at the appraisal interview, you can now begin the process of turning the tables – manoeuvring the appraisal to get out of it what *you* want.

thinking smart

BE ASSERTIVE

Don't go into the appraisal interview cowed or beaten. Go in assertive and upbeat. Be confident and know what it is you want from this interview – that's the next bit. You must turn the tables, so to speak, so that it is you who is in charge of this interview. It isn't being conducted for the benefit of your boss so they can just slag you off or pat you on the back. They might like to think this is the case but the clever team member – that's you, remember – will demand a lot more from it, manipulate it so you get from it exactly what you want and use it as a valuable weapon in your business armoury.

And what, pray, is it that you want? Well, this can usually be broken down into three key areas:

- **things needed for promotion**
- **things needed for pay rises**
- **things needed for personal satisfaction.**

Let's have a quick look at each of these as time is short and tomorrow creeps ever nearer.

Things needed for promotion. If you are going to ask for things needed for promotion – training, increased responsibilities, new skills, extra duties, that sort of thing – you have to have a career plan. You have to know exactly where you expect to be in six months, a year, two years and five years. You have to know where you're going and how you expect to get there. Too often we sort of muddle along and let things take their course. But not you, not the smart team member. You will know, arrow like, exactly where you are going. All you have to do is plan what it is you need for the next step up and ask accordingly. Your appraisal interview is the place to discuss these career steps and find out what your boss thinks.

Things needed for pay rises. The appraisal interview is a good place to do a little Machiavellian scheming. If you want a pay rise you have to justify it, you have to be worth more. Ask your boss what you can do to be worth more. They may say, '*Oh, learn the new ZX35 and you'll be entitled to a supplement,*' or '*Simple really, by supervising the new recruit for six months and making sure they understand the new invoicing system you'll be worth an extra £X a year.*' Then all you'll have to do is make sure these things happen and go back and do an Oliver. Your boss will find it very hard to turn down your request for more, seeing as how they set you up for the pay rise in the first place. Clever, huh?

Things needed for personal satisfaction. Your company may be big or small but chances are it has the wherewithal and resources for you to further your personal skills and knowledge. Gaining new skills may not directly affect your promotion or pay increase chances but they may do a lot to further your personal satisfaction. You may be a marketing manager who is fascinated by sales, so it wouldn't hurt you to learn some of the strategies associated with this field. It may not directly affect you but it is interesting to see how other departments function, as well as furthering your understanding of the business as a whole. Or perhaps you might ask for a chance to launch a newsletter for your department and request some training if you haven't a clue about setting one up. This doesn't directly affect your chances of promotion or a pay rise but it certainly shows you are committed and willing – and you get to learn a lot of valuable new skills.

You can also bring up other factors such as:

- working conditions
- hours
- working from home
- relationships with colleagues
- canteen facilities
- inter-departmental relationships
- social functions and facilities
- health issues
- equipment resources.

SEEING THE BIGGER PICTURE

By broadening your horizons and seeing how your industry works, you get to see the bigger picture. This will stand you in good stead when it comes to seeing how other departments cause you and your department problems. Once you understand how they operate you can be more forgiving, more amenable and more understanding.

If there is something you'd really like to learn or understand and it isn't entirely within the remit of your job, it is OK to ask at your appraisal interview. It shows you have a quick and lively mind and are willing to expand and grow – no bad thing when it comes to being seen as helpful and cooperative, keen *and* useful. Jobsworths don't get promoted very often but the 'I can do that' types certainly do.

FOR NEXT TIME

At the appraisal interview your boss has access to your personnel file. You should keep your own. Keep a file in which you log any incidents of an unusual nature, along with your successes, failures, strengths and weaknesses. This way there will be no surprises at the appraisal as you will have the same sort of record – the same song sheet – your boss has. You can do a quick recap and be on top of the situation. You will have forgotten nothing and thus not have to have your memory jogged about something, which always looks bad.

Ask well in advance for your pre-appraisal preparation document so you have lots of time to fill it in. In fact you can start to fill it in, mentally, before you've even received it. Know what the last six months or year have been like and be ready to answer all the questions. Have a plan worked out in advance of what you want and what you need.

All you have to do is plan what it is you need for the next step up and ask accordingly

3 the interview environment

The clock is ticking and there are only so many hours left before tomorrow and your own appraisal – and you still have all your usual work to do as well. We'd better move fast, but efficiently. We need to have a look at what you are likely to expect tomorrow in the way of an interview environment – and ways of turning it to your advantage.

Now there are some places – and ways – where it is inappropriate to be interviewed and you have the right to ask for a postponement if someone tries to subject you to such a thing. An appraisal should never, under any circumstances, be conducted:

- ▶ **in or next to the work's canteen**
- ▶ **in a corridor**
- ▶ **in an open-plan office**
- ▶ **in front of colleagues**
- ▶ **at home**

- **on the shop floor**
- **over the phone**
- **by e-mail or fax.**

And in an ideal world you should never be interviewed in your boss's office because:

- **it isn't neutral enough and you may feel intimidated – a bit like entering the lion's den**
- **your boss may find it more difficult staving off interruptions**
- **your boss might be distracted and get up to close the filing cabinet or see a file that was in their pending tray and suddenly think of a note to add – that sort of thing.**

So where? Well, most organisations keep an interview room for just such purposes. Your boss should, if they know the game, ask to borrow a colleague's office rather than use their own. A conference room or even the board room at a pinch would be suitable. You need somewhere quiet, away from interruptions, neutral and with the right sort of seating. You need to know you won't be turfed out unexpectedly or have people poking their heads round the door every five minutes to see who is using the room.

You need somewhere you can feel is a relaxed and informal atmosphere so perhaps the board room isn't ideal after all. Your boss may not be intimidated as they may be used to using such a room, but you may well be uncomfortable, and even if you're not, that possibility should have been taken into consideration.

NOISE AND INTERRUPTIONS

A quiet meeting room should have been supplied, well away from the hurly burly of office life. If the builders are in next door, don't try to shout above the noise – ask to move rooms. Make sure a notice requesting no interruptions, and with a finish time on it, has been posted on the outside of the door. If it hasn't, then ask for it to be done.

thinking fast

LIGHTING

You must have adequate light to see clearly and be able to make notes. Check any spotlights and make sure they're not behind your boss and shining in your face. If they are, ask for them to be angled away or you may well end up thinking you're helping the police with their inquiries. If the lighting is too dim ask for it to be turned up – or down if it is too bright.

thinking smart

NO PHONES

Switch off your mobile phone, your bleeper and your pager, and make sure you're not interrupted by internal phones ringing for you. Tell everyone in your department that you are away from your desk for an hour and are not to be interrupted. Your boss should have done the same so the two of you should be left in peace. Your appraisal should be very high up your boss's priority list and being interrupted to sign something or to be asked where something is can send out the wrong message to you – a valued team member.

The key factors to take into consideration when being interviewed somewhere are:

- **confidentiality**
- **peace and quiet**
- **distractions**
- **furnishing and seating**
- **light.**

You should have the respect paid to you to have had a special room provided with all these factors taken into consideration. If any feel wrong then you

If the builders are in next door, don't try to shout above the noise – ask to move rooms

have the right to ask for a change of venue or a postponement if that is not possible.

SEATING ARRANGEMENTS

If you get a chance, pop along and check out the room where your interview is going to take place. It helps if you've had a quick look beforehand so you won't find it strange or intimidating when you go in – forewarned is forearmed. Have a look at the seating arrangement. There are five basic seating arrangements for such an assessment and each one carries its own message and has benefits or drawbacks:

- You both sit in low chairs round a coffee table.
- You sit at opposite ends of a meeting table.
- Your boss sits behind a desk and you sit facing them from the other side.
- You both sit in office chairs on the same side of the desk.
- You sit next to each other at a meeting table.

We talked earlier of turning the tables. Now you can put this into practice, literally perhaps. There is nothing to stop you taking control and suggesting where you sit. Unless your boss has a very rigid mind-set and is very formal you might well be able to lead the interview by suggesting a seating arrangement that you will both find relaxing, informal, constructive and pleasing. Let's have a quick look at how seating can change the tone and atmosphere of an appraisal.

You both sit in low chairs round a coffee table. This is certainly comfortable but it is impractical for making notes as you have to bend forward or keep getting up to look at files. The table itself may be too small.

You sit at opposite ends of a meeting table. This is good as you can both spread out papers in front of you but it is slightly too formal and slightly confrontational.

Your boss sits behind a desk and you sit facing them from the other side. Very formal, very confrontational. Hopefully your boss will have read *fast thinking: appraisal* and will avoid it at all costs.

You both sit in office chairs on the same side of a desk. Informal but not very comfortable. One of you gets to rest an elbow on the desk but the other has nowhere to spread papers.

You sit next to each other at a meeting table. Very good indeed. It is informal and friendly and practical. Ideally one of you should sit at the short end and the other just around the corner on the long side. If you sit right next to each other it is harder to achieve eye contact (very important) and you have the feeling the other is looking over your shoulder all the time.

So what should you suggest or choose? Well, the next to each other but at right angles approach is

thinking fast

REFRESHMENTS AND BREAKS

A cup of coffee or tea is always welcome and helps break the ice. Hopefully you'll be offered one to settle you into the right sort of relaxed approach. If you do get asked make sure you say 'Yes please' and don't ask for anything that obviously isn't available like a decaf cappuccino with a sweetener if it is clear that there is only instant with white sugar. You are entitled to ask for a break to use the lavatory but try to go beforehand so there is no break and the whole thing flows easily from one topic to another. The process should be informal so you can ask to have your jacket off or whatever appeals to you to feel more comfortable. If, for any reason, the discussion becomes heated then ask for a break so you can both calm down: 'Can we just take a five minute break here so I can collect my thoughts?'

the best. Take the lead here and allow your boss the 'head of table' position out of respect – you can take the lead but don't dominate. It's easy to manipulate this one – just go and sit down and say, 'Is it all right if I sit here, then?' Not many bosses will argue as it is obvious you are being helpful, keen and enthusiastic. What more could they ask?

This is what it looks like:

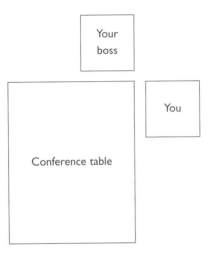

If there isn't a meeting table, choose another seating arrangement but avoid sitting opposite each other as this is more formal and can be confrontational.

WOOING A CLIENT

Try to create the same sort of atmosphere as you would to woo a client if you deal with them. You're not here to be interrogated or disciplined. It is an informal-style business meeting between two colleagues, one of whom happens to be senior to the other. Treat your boss in much the same way as you would one of your clients – be respectful but friendly, informal but not too chatty.

WHAT TO TAKE WITH YOU

Make sure you have a copy of the memo stating when and where, and that you have checked you are on time and at the right place. Take a copy with you of your pre-appraisal preparation document. You can also take with you any additional information such as a letter from a client praising your services, a written apology from the member of your team involved in that unfortunate incident with the two book-keepers and the ice-making machine (you may be asked about the incident and what you did about it), copies of successful orders, details of training courses you want to attend, a list of questions you want to ask, your own version of your personnel file (see previous chapter), and anything else that you feel you might need for discussion.

Make sure you have it all in a smart folder and that you have a pen with you. There is nothing worse than having to ask to borrow your boss's pen to make notes – which means they can't use it while you've got it.

for next time

Make sure you make it well known that, if last time the meeting place was wrong or inappropriate, you warrant better treatment this time. This can be done in a very light-hearted way. Merely say to your boss when they give you the memo telling you when your appraisal is, 'Oh, we're not having it in the canteen again, are we?' and then laugh as if the very idea is ridiculous. If your boss asks what is wrong with that, then tell them: lack of confidentiality, no freedom from interruption, unsuitable and too noisy.

You have to treat this matter with the respect it deserves and if that means manipulating a little bit, then so be it. Your appraisal warrants the best place, the best atmosphere and the best of attention. Don't settle for second best.

Make sure you've got all your notes together in time and have kept your own personnel file up to date.

4 the structure and agenda

W ell, we're moving along at a terrific pace but there is still no time to lose. We have to think and act at the speed of life if we are to get through the rest of this and have you come up smelling of roses at that appraisal tomorrow – and we will.

THE INFORMAL FORMAL MEETING

So, tomorrow is an informal formal meeting, if you get my drift. Notes will be taken, minutes even, an action plan will be formulated. Yep, it's a formal meeting all right and yet informal in the sense that it will be just the two of you and thus chatty and friendly, casual even – informal. But still a meeting. And what do you need for a meeting? That's right, an agenda.

Now, who sets this agenda? Given that there are only the two of you there should be no need for this agenda to be too heavy. Nor should it be imposed on you from above. Nor should it be too detailed. But there should be an agenda and there should be a structure to the meeting.

THE JOINT AGENDA

And the best time to set such an agenda? Why, tomorrow of course, at the meeting. And whose job is it to set such an agenda? Why, it's a joint thing, you both do. However, out of courtesy to your boss you let them set the pace, start the ball rolling so to speak. *Your* job is to make sure that everything *you* want discussed gets included – and in the right order. You could see your appraisal as a

thinking smart

YOUR JOB DESCRIPTION

Some team members think their job description is a sort of set of rules – something they have to stick to rigidly. But you can go beyond the call of your job description – do more in fact. Your appraisal interview is the place to point out these extensions in a tactful way. You're not asking for praise or a pat on the back. You are merely pointing out that you are the 'I can do that' type. When the next promotion comes round you'll be remembered and thought of favourably, rather than as a jobsworth.

You could see your appraisal as a story – a tale being told to you – and like all good stories it should have a beginning, a middle and an end story – a tale being told to you – and like all good stories it should have a beginning, a middle and an end.

If your boss has read *fast thinking: appraisal* they'll know the format, which might be useful for you to know so you understand where they're coming from – and why.

The programme usually takes roughly this form:

1. They should spend a moment or two putting you at your ease – offering you a cup of tea, showing you where you can sit, asking you about your children/new car/hobbies – that sort of thing. This is designed to relax you and make you feel comfortable. Go along with it and be friendly, answer questions in a light-hearted manner (don't be suspicious if they ask something about you, it is to make you feel comfortable and isn't a trap or test).

2. They'll signal that the 'chat' is over and it is time to get on with the real reason you are there. This may take the form of them saying something like, 'Now, let's get down to business, shall we?' Of course you say, 'Yes'.

3. They'll explain what the meeting is about: 'So, as you know this is your six-monthly appraisal.' Of course you know, but they say it just to fix it firmly in both your minds – there can be no misunderstanding if it has been said out loud. They are not patronising you, merely putting a title at the top of the page.

4. They should then outline a framework of what is going to happen: 'I thought we'd have a look at how the job has been going, then we'll have a look in detail at a couple of things I would like to bring up, then we'll see if there's anything you'd like to talk about, a quick look at training and then we'll wrap it up, OK?'

And this last point is where most team members nod meekly and the appraisal begins. But not you, oh no, not you. You are the smart thinker, the fast thinker. And this is where you strike, cobra-like, to take control of the appraisal and turn it to your advantage. You don't nod or mumble, 'That'll be fine.' You start on a positive note: 'Sounds good. But may I make a suggestion?' Of course your boss agrees, they can do nothing else as they have already asked you if it's OK and have thus put themselves in a position where you can contribute.

YOUR OWN AGENDA

Now what is your suggestion going to be? Well, that depends entirely on what you want to achieve at this appraisal. You should have worked out an agenda of your own in advance – that means today by the way: time is running out and you have to get a move on and get it done now. So what is your agenda? Well, you should say something like this (with the reasons why in brackets):

1. 'Well, firstly I'd like to work through the pre-appraisal preparation document and see what you thought of my answers. It's important to me to check that we both agree that my performance has been up to standard.' (This makes sure you are both singing from the same song sheet and stops the pre-appraisal preparation document getting ignored or overlooked, which it can do in the heat of battle, so to speak.)

2. 'Then we could discuss the points you'd like to raise with me.' (Give them their chance to have a say – after all they are the boss and what they want to raise could well be interesting, informative or beneficial to you.)

3. 'I've also got a few points to raise about the new invoicing system which I feel we could discuss, and I would like to ask a couple of questions about the move to Shrewsbury and how that is going to affect my department in the long term.' (This is your chance to get everything clear; anything you are unsure about can be raised here.)

4. 'And finally I really would like to discuss some training ideas I have regarding the new ZX35 and I've got a couple of ideas for some things which aren't directly connected with my job but I'd really like your advice on.' (Now you can bring up any training needs you have or anything else you might like information on such as running that new newsletter. And you've flattered them a bit.)

Now what you have suggested is pretty much what they suggested. But the roles have changed. Instead of being passive you have become much more proactive. You have:

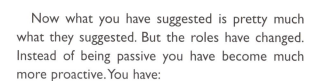 stamped your mark firmly but fairly on this appraisal

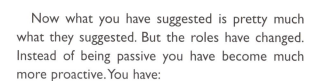 made it very clear that you have a valuable input

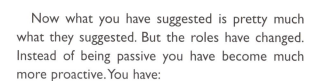 shown that it is a joint process

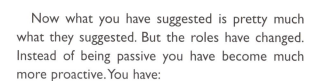 stressed that you have bright and good ideas and want them to be taken seriously

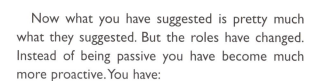 shown that you have taken some time and trouble over this appraisal and regard it as important

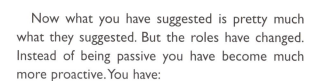 made it clear that you are no pushover and that you are intelligent and smart.

LET THEM TAKE A BACK SEAT

Not bad at all and all you did is ask if you could make a mere suggestion. There aren't many bosses who would react badly to this. Most, if not all, will be pleased that you have taken so much interest, will be happy to take a back seat and let you run your own appraisal and will be impressed with your skills at running a meeting.

11

PUT YOURSELF IN THEIR SHOES

If you hold appraisals yourself, notice what makes an appraisal 'easy' or 'difficult'. What does the team member do that makes it flow or feel awkward? Try to adopt good tactics – the same ones your team members adopt with you that makes it 'easy', makes it 'flow' – with your boss. By making it easy on them you get remembered as a 'good' team member, which earns brownie points for later.

WHO'S RUNNING THIS APPRAISAL?

By now you should have this appraisal firmly in hand and your boss should be sitting up and taking notice. There are a couple of other things you can do to make sure they know who is running this appraisal:

- ▶ **Take notes. Don't just do this but ask politely if it's OK to do so. They can't not let you – just so long as you have your own pen of course. It keeps them on their toes if they know anything they say is being taken down and may be used in evidence against them. Take the top off your pen and have a note pad ready to use. This looks terribly professional and business-like – you have come prepared and are ready and willing.**

- Open your folder and arrange your papers neatly in front of you. Let them see if you have brochures about training courses, education packages or research projects. You can put them to one side but it sets the tone of the meeting and shows that you have important things to discuss later on.

- Finish your tea and discreetly move the cup well away from you. This signals that the chatty, informal bit is over and you are ready to settle down to the serious business of the meeting.

- Sit up straight and make good eye contact – but don't stare. Look alert and lean slightly forward as if you are ready to hang on their every word. Which of course you are, as what they have to say directly affects your job, your career, your working life, your promotion prospects, your pay rises, your future and your work satisfaction levels. They may not have realised all this and thought they were merely doing a six-monthly appraisal.

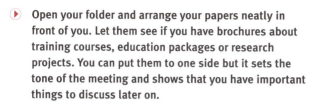

thinking smart

THE HANDSHAKE

Your handshake is one of those unconscious signals that is so important to get right. The firm, strong handshake signals a firm strong team member. The limp wet fish signals exactly that. Get a friend to tell you what your handshake tells people about you – and change it if the message isn't what you would like to give.

THANK THEM

Now all you've got to do is have the appraisal and wrap it up. Pretty easy. Make sure you agree with any summary at the end of the meeting and you have both made the same notes as to who is doing what. We'll go through the actual appraisal in the next section and what you should say and how you should say it.

thinking fast

NOT SIGNING

At the end of the appraisal you may be asked to sign a form that says you have had your appraisal and that you are happy with everything that's been said. This isn't a trap or a test but merely a way of recording for future reference that everything that should be done has been done. But what if you don't agree? What if your boss says you've been inefficient, work-shy, disruptive, uncooperative? What do you do? You think fast, that's what you do.

You say 'I would like to take away a copy of this and just check it over before signing. There are a couple of points I'd like to think about before signing. I take it that's OK?' Then the ball's in their court. They can demand you sign at which juncture you can refuse point blank (but politely). Or they'll ask what points need clarification and you get a chance to air your views and make it clear that you disagree with their assessment of your work performance. Either way you haven't signed something you disagree with and you have assertively but fairly made your stand.

Just before you go thank them for the appraisal – it may be part of their job to do it and part of your job to receive it but thank them anyway and make sure it sounds sincere. They'll remember this and look forward to the next one with you.

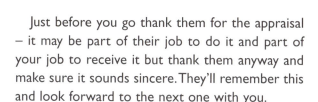

for next time

If you are going to request any extra training or education programmes make sure you have done your research in advance. Have the necessary information to hand to discuss or for your boss to take away with them – brochures, catalogues, promotional material, leaflets. It makes your case a lot easier to sell if you can provide costs, timescales, benefits etc.

Work out in advance what agenda you want – what you want the appraisal to achieve – rather than taking the passive approach of accepting what is said without contributing. Work out a logical order, a structure that makes sense and pretty well fits in with the sort of structure your boss will want to impose. It is easier to guide gently than wrestle for control and steer violently in a totally new direction.

5 what are you going to say?

Nearly there but we still have a lot of ground to cover so no slacking, keep up and stay ahead of the game. We've looked at the preparation you'll need, your input into the interview environment and how to structure the agenda. Now we need to have a look at what you are actually going to say – and how you are going to say it. Yep, there is a right way and lots of wrong ways of putting across your ideas. Get it wrong and you risk putting your boss's back up, making a fool of yourself, failing to communicate effectively and ending up with the wrong sort of action plan – or worse, a bad appraisal that will live on in your personnel file to haunt you for years to come. Get it right and you come across as business-like, efficient, smart, quick and simply brilliant.

ALL BOSSES ARE DIFFERENT

As well as what you are going to say, and how you are going to say it, we also need to look at who you are going to say it to. Yes, I know it's your boss. But bosses are all different and there are some holy terrors out there that need to be handled very carefully. Hopefully yours is an absolute sweetheart who has read all the *fast thinking* guides – even invested in the manual – but they may not be. They may be inept, too busy, dominant or perhaps even under-assertive. So let's look at these types and the best techniques for handling them before we look at what to say. If we know who we are saying it to it might be easier to tailor what we are going to say. So, the main difficult types are:

- ▶ the boss who's too busy
- ▶ the inept boss
- ▶ the dominant boss
- ▶ the under-assertive boss
- ▶ the unorganised boss
- ▶ the uninterested boss
- ▶ the misdirected boss.

There are a lot of other types as well but they are usually in subsets of the ones above. So as well as learning specific techniques for dealing with the main ones we'll look at ways of fast thinking to deal with any that crop up that we haven't covered. Once you get into the swing of handling difficult bosses it's easy to stay one jump ahead. Let's look now at the specific techniques. But quick, those little grains of sand are running out of your personal hour glass and tomorrow looms large. We shall have a lot to do and time and tide wait for none of us.

The boss who's too busy

They want an easy life and aren't prepared to make an effort. An appraisal to them is just another chore to be got through and the less they do the better they think it is. They simply don't have enough time in the day to get through their work and that's without the bother of your appraisal.

You'll have to be quite assertive to deal with the too-busy boss. Ten minutes into your appraisal they may suddenly remember they have an urgent appointment with the CEO and have to fly. 'Sorry and all that but I simply have to go, have a quick sign here to say you've had your appraisal and I'll see you in six months, OK?' No, it's not OK. You'll have to stand firm, stand your ground. Explain that you haven't discussed anything you wanted to and could you please re-schedule this appraisal for another time. Politely but firmly refuse to sign to say you've had your appraisal if you feel you haven't. Don't give in or back down because you are being pressured by time constraints or a too-busy boss. A decent appraisal is your right and without it you are missing out on a valuable and vital part of your work toolkit.

The inept boss

This type of manager basically hasn't a clue. They don't bother reading *fast thinking* guides (shame!), training themselves, improving their skills or investing in good team relations. The sad thing is they often don't know they are inept, which makes it worse. They're the type to hold an appraisal in the staff canteen because they don't know any better.

They are usually quite easy to rein in, bring back under control. When they suggest the canteen merely say, 'Oh, I'm not sure that's a good idea. I'm sure we would want more privacy and it wouldn't be very comfortable for us, would it?' If you set the

They're the type to hold an appraisal in the staff canteen because they don't know any better

lead, they'll follow. Because they are unsure of themselves or the way things work they'll usually be very glad of your experience and expertise and allow you to set them straight. They are woolly thinkers and your clarity will seem like a godsend to them. Just so long as you don't overdo it and take over they are usually a pushover. Talk in terms of 'we' rather than 'I'. Once they know you know what you are doing they'll be happy to take a back seat and let you drive. Just don't let them set the agenda or organise anything.

The dominant boss

They know what's best for you. They try to impose their will, their way, their methods on any meeting or interview – including yours tomorrow. They believe they are infallible, invincible and ultimately right.

This is the tough one to handle. They know they are right so what could you possibly tell them that would change their minds? Answer? Nothing at all. You would be wasting your time. But because this boss is so sure of themselves they have a big ego – and what better way is there of manipulating the big ego? That's right, by flattery. Don't tell them anything, ask instead. Ask for their advice, their views, their opinions. If you need to discuss training needs ask them how you should approach this. We know you've got it all worked out and know exactly what training course you need to go on and where and how. But by asking their advice you'll quickly get them on your side. Then you can gently steer things round to your way of thinking, again by the flattery approach. Show them your brochures, details, leaflets and ask them what they think. Lots of 'So, do you think this would be good for me?' and, 'I'd really value your help here. Which course would be best for me?' The dominant boss is only dominant because they are covering up some deficiency. Once you realise what that is – and the same goes for any other difficult boss – you can work with it. Once you see what they are hiding you know their weaknesses and vulnerabilities. And thus you can manipulate the situation to your own advantage.

The under-assertive boss

These managers are frightened to make a decision in case it is wrong, frightened to apply any constructive criticism in case you think badly of them, terrified to take charge, take control or take a risk. They may even be worried about you taking their job so they may want you to be seen in a bad light, just in case.

The two types – the under-assertive because they are frightened and the under-assertive because they are worried – need slightly different handling. The frightened boss just needs to know that you are in charge and they can relax. Once they trust you – and you will gently encourage this because you are good at it – you can do what you like with them. The worried under-assertive boss mustn't be startled into thinking you are more skilled than them. You need to make sure they think you are in awe of them and wouldn't dream of being able to take their job. Make sure they think you are part of the team and without them you can't make a decision or wipe your nose properly. You do this by asking for their help, their support and their sustenance. Make sure they think you need them.

The unorganised boss

They forget to bring your file with them, forget that they were even doing an appraisal today, forget which room it is being held in. Their lack of organisation can spill over onto you and make you look similarly unorganised if you don't watch it.

This difficult boss is much easier to handle. You just become their nursemaid. Phone them just before the appraisal interview and say, 'Oh, just checking I've got it right, it is 3 o'clock in the downstairs meeting room, isn't it?' That way you've gently reminded them and made sure they know where as well. You can go further and ask, 'Is there anything I need to bring, such as my personnel file? Oh no, silly me, you bring that of course.' Just don't make it too obvious.

The uninterested boss

They can't be bothered quite frankly. They've had to do a lot of appraisals lately and they've switched off, become bored and are mentally elsewhere.

Again an easy boss to switch back on. Make the appraisal interesting for them. Ask loads of questions and fire them up with enthusiasm by

thinking fast

TALK OF 'WE'

In an appraisal you will find you get a better response if you talk in terms of 'we' rather than 'I'. For instance, 'It would be helpful if we had a better understanding of the new invoicing procedures', rather than 'I haven't got a clue about the new invoices.' The 'we' in this example includes the whole of your department and stops you looking stupid in isolation.

being big and bold, dramatic and stylish. Entertain them. Make them laugh if necessary. Make an impact. Bring a little light and colour into their drab world and you'll get and keep their interest.

The misdirected boss

This type of boss will always see the appraisal interview as a useful opportunity to be used for other purposes – the disciplinary interview, the training session, the pay review, the discussion about next year's marketing plans, a budget review – whatever. They get lost along the way – they have been misdirected.

You'll have to redirect them. When they try and turn the appraisal into a disciplinary interview or whatever, remind them gently by saying, 'Oh, I didn't think we were here for that. I'm sorry but you've caught me totally unprepared. I haven't any notes or anything. Could we set aside some time later for that when I'll be better organised?' If they insist you may have to insist as well: 'Look, this is my appraisal and I'd like to get on with it properly. If we can't then could we re-schedule it for another time? I'm happy to discuss the incident with the catering supervisor and the custard but I thought it had been dealt with. Do you mean this is an official disciplinary hearing/budget review/training session/ whatever?' Stress the *official* and they'll back down; they know deep down they shouldn't be using your appraisal time to talk about other things – it's very, very naughty of them.

So, you've got the hang of it now. (A good source of information on this is to be found in *fast thinking: difficult people*.) We have to get a move on, that clock is ticking.

WHAT TO SAY

So what are you going to say? Obviously your boss is going to want to go through your appraisal making comments about your work and your performance. These comments, ideally, if they have

thinking smart

WHOSE APPRAISAL IS IT?

Don't use your appraisal to attack, or even discuss, your boss's managerial style or incompetence. It is your appraisal and should be treated as such. They may be a disorganised old duffer who hasn't a clue but it is not your job to point that out or try to correct it. Hopefully their own weaknesses will be picked up at *their* appraisal – but yours is not the place to do it.

read *fast thinking: appraisal*, will be about your job and not about you. It's a subtle difference but it is important to make you feel that this appraisal is fair and objective. For instance, they could say, 'You haven't been working well,' or they could say, 'The job hasn't been completed well.' The first will make you defensive and put your back up, the second will allow you to explain that you didn't get the resources you needed or there was some other problem that stopped you working as effectively as you could have. But what are you going to say? I do hope you're not going to sit there like a frightened rabbit and just accept everything and have nothing to give back. Some team members do and their appraisal is as good as worthless to both them and their boss. It achieves nothing. Much better to have worked out in advance how you are going to respond to any aspect of your job that is going to be brought up.

In an ideal world

You are going to say everything you need to, to validate, to explain and to justify — assuming you have to, of course. In an ideal world you will go in tomorrow and they will compliment you on every aspect of your job and you will simply glow with pride. Get real. It ain't like that. None of us is perfect. What is more likely to happen is that certain parts of your job where you haven't been as efficient as you might have been will be highlighted, while all the brilliant bits will be skated over far too quickly. Most bosses see an appraisal as the one place where they can really tighten up on all your weak spots while ignoring the essential praise.

'It's not my fault'

What are you going to say? Well, one thing you are not going to say is, 'It wasn't my fault'. Not under any circumstances. Even if it wasn't. What you are going to say is, 'Good point. I can entirely see why you think that. However, there are a couple of factors I feel you ought to take into consideration. For instance, it was actually Bob who signed off the report sheets which incurred this massive expense. I was in Birmingham at the time and didn't get to hear about it until after I got back. Once I returned I carried out the rescue plan as we discussed and the vital components were returned to us, remanufactured and redelivered in record time. The client was happy and although we did lose money we shall make that up on the next order which the client has already indicated will be forthcoming.'

You will go in tomorrow and they will compliment you on every aspect of your job and you will simply glow with pride. Get real. It ain't like that

COUNSELLING TECHNIQUES

It is smart thinking to use counselling techniques at your appraisal. Instead of saying, 'I get really cheesed off when you dump extra work on me,' to which the standard reply is invariably, 'Tough, that's what you're paid for,' try saying, 'Is there any way I could feel better about all the extra work that gets given to me at the last minute?' You'll be soliciting a response that has to be helpful because you have phrased it right. Try not to say, 'When you do … I feel …' This implies it is their fault. Instead, reverse it: 'I feel … when I am …' And then ask if there might be any way you could feel better or less put upon or less pressured or taken for granted, such as, 'I feel that I am under too much pressure when work is given to me at the last minute. Is there any way we could ease this situation?' Much better than, 'You give me too much work at the last minute and I'm fed up with it.'

By using a counselling technique and not apportioning blame you'll get further more easily – now *that's* thinking smart.

Whingey and snivelling

See. There is a difference. You could have said, 'But it wasn't my fault. Bob did it.' In one way you are seen as competent and business-like whereas the other way you are seen as whingey and snivelling.

What you are going to say is going to be:

- clear
- concise
- objective
- intelligent
- calm
- non-emotive
- reasoned
- thought out in advance
- backed up with facts.

Measuring your performance

If they say you haven't performed well, don't rise to the bait. Ask them, 'In what areas?' or, 'Could you be more specific?' or even, 'How do you mean "well"?' Get them to define it clearly. Get them to lay it out in front of you. You can't discuss generalities such as 'You haven't performed as well as I would have liked.' There are simply too many variables and undefined areas there. Your performance must be measured against certain standards. If you fall short you can be corrected. If you come up to scratch you can be praised. But your performance has to be measurable and not

One thing you are not going to say is, 'It wasn't my fault'. Not under any circumstances. Even if it wasn't

judged on opinion. You must be given specifics and have the right to ask for them.

If you're not happy, say so

This is what you are going to say. You are going to ask – not demand – that any criticism is supported with evidence, facts, specific incidents, times, places, dates – that sort of thing. We will look at receiving constructive criticism in the next chapter but for now remember that you are no rabbit and can ask for anything you want. If you are not happy then say so: 'I'm not happy that you see me as work-shy and lazy. I can't defend such an accusation if you don't give me specific examples or show me where my work has fallen short of my targets.' That'll fox 'em.

What you also need to say is that you want a clear and objective appraisal of your work performance in terms of your:

- overall approach to work
- motivation
- strengths and weaknesses
- acceptance of responsibility
- supervisory capacities
- technical knowledge

- ▶ planning, organising and co-ordinating abilities
- ▶ team qualities
- ▶ areas for improvement
- ▶ training/guidance/instruction (i.e. required by you)
- ▶ long-term goals.

Anything less than this is not a full and comprehensive appraisal. Without this information you can't hope to proceed to the next stages of your career.

HOW TO SAY IT

So now we know *what* you are going to say, how are you going to say it? Easy. There are a few rules for discussing anything at an appraisal interview – or any other interview come to that.

- ▶ Be calm.
- ▶ Be friendly.
- ▶ Maintain eye contact.
- ▶ Be specific, objective and focused on the job in hand.
- ▶ Don't get defensive, and don't fold your arms as that gives the impression that you are on the defensive.
- ▶ Don't get angry.

You are going to ask – not demand – that any criticism is supported with evidence, facts, specific incidents, times, places, dates

- Lean forward to indicate you are paying attention.

- Don't get personal, abusive or threatening.

- Don't whinge or moan.

- Ask, don't demand.

Open and closed answers

If your boss asks your opinion of something – anything, your job performance, the weather, the success of the new invoicing system – there are two ways of answering – the open answer and the closed answer. You will use the open format and not the closed. No, we're not going to argue. You have your mission – use open answers only. Now let's do it. What's that? You don't know what an open answer is? Or a closed one? OK, we'll look at a couple of examples and I'll explain why you're going to use the open version.

So your boss asks, 'How's the job going?' A closed answer is the one-word variety, 'Fine.'

Let's try it again with the open version. 'How's the job going?' 'Fine, I'm quite pleased with the progress I'm making with the ZX35 but could do with a little more help on the packaging design brief. There's a couple of points I'd like to make about the new parking arrangements but I guess we'll get round to that in a minute.'

You've proved yourself to be a good communicator, interested in your job, prepared to admit there are areas you need help with and easy and responsive to talk to. Award yourself 10 brownie points. The first (closed) answer above would have revealed you as a sullen hostile team member who would probably rather be somewhere else. Deduct 15 brownie points for this answer.

This open technique works for any question or statement fired at you. 'Awful weather, isn't it?' says the boss as you all gather round the coffee machine in the morning. 'Yes,' reply the sullen ones, but you say, 'Yes, must play havoc with your garden at this time of year. Have your begonias suffered much?' Boss mentally awards you brownie points and deducts from others.

Remember:

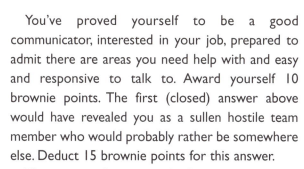

- **An open question *opens* up discussion – it needs a response.**

- **A closed answer *closes* it down – it doesn't encourage a response.**

The last thing that you want to do at your appraisal is close down discussion. And once you've mastered this technique you'll look good,

There are two ways of answering – the open answer and the closed answer.

You will use the open format and not the closed

appear business-like and efficient, and come across as someone who really knows their onions – not bad at all. Next we'll look at ways of improving your performance – or ways of suggesting you do so – and handling constructive criticism. Let's rock and roll.

for next time

Make sure you have genned up on difficult bosses well in advance and know which sort – if any – yours is. There are ways of handling them all without them realising (don't let them read this), and ways of turning the tables so it is you who is running this appraisal.

Make sure you have clearly fixed in your mind what you want this appraisal to achieve and that you are prepared to go for it.

Practise your interview techniques so you get it right, get it good. Be confident at all times and you'll come across as someone who knows what they are talking about – which of course you do.

6 accepting constructive criticism

OK, let's get on with it. Not far to go now but we really must make haste if we are to get you ready for this appraisal tomorrow – and have you looking good. Now we need to have a quick look at the best ways of handling constructive criticism. The whole point of an appraisal is not just to pat you kindly on the back, tell you that you are doing a great job and send you on your way feeling great. Oh, no. Your appraisal – and you should be thankful for this bit – is also to point out your weak areas and find ways of improving them.

LOST!

If we don't know where we are going wrong we may carry on getting more and more lost, diverging more and more from the right path. By having our weaknesses pointed out we stand a good chance of getting back on track quickly and effectively before too much damage is done to our career. That's why it is essential to have these appraisals at short and regular intervals such as six months which, quite frankly, is the minimum you deserve. Leaving them as long as a year – or even two years – is just too long. That would be a bit like looking at the map just as you leave home on a long and strange journey and then never bothering again – you could end up in Carlisle when you were going to Bristol.

CONSTRUCTIVE CRITICISM

And the best way of getting you back on track is by *constructive* criticism. Note the word *constructive* by the way. It involves never pointing out a weakness without suggesting a way of correcting it, never highlighting a problem without suggesting the solution. Your boss telling you that you are crap at something isn't helpful, it isn't constructive. Them telling you that you're not much cop at something and then telling you why and offering additional training to improve matters is much better (all bosses take note here).

Before you can have the weakness corrected it has to be mentioned and discussed. You have to be given an opportunity to justify or explain why you think that particular area is a weak one for you. And you have to be given an opportunity to suggest ways you think you could improve. If all the recommendations come down to you from on high you won't value them as much as if you were also involved in the discussion process – you have to feel involved to want to put in the effort to correct it. Besides which, ideas imposed on you from on high may simply not work for you anyway – you want to do the spreadsheet course and they think you would be better off learning pest control even though you're the finance officer.

thinking smart

DON'T GIVE THEM INFORMATION INDIGESTION

If you've done your job properly you will have gathered together all the brochures or leaflets or details of any training courses you want to go on. Make a sort of mini presentation out of them. List the details and benefits on one sheet of A4 and let them ask if they want to see more. Don't expect them to pore over all of them and be as interested as you are. And don't bombard them with information. Select the course you want and have the information to hand but don't overload your boss with details.

HOW ARE YOU GOING TO REACT?

So tomorrow you are going to have to face up to the fact that some things you do will fall short of the expected standards and that you are going to be told about it. So how are you going to react? There are some responses which are inappropriate:

- anger
- defensiveness
- sulkiness
- disagreement
- meek acceptance
- argument
- transferring the blame onto someone else.

What is appropriate is:

- listening attentively
- regarding this as an opportunity to improve, and being grateful
- being prepared to discuss things reasonably and calmly and intelligently.

Much easier than the other responses. Now *how* your boss decides to tell you is another matter.

We'll assume they know what they are doing and tell you in the right way. This usually involves pointing out the fault or weak area, then allowing a discussion, and finally offering ways and means of doing it better and jointly deciding on a policy. That's *jointly* remember.

No surprises

Your appraisal should contain no surprises. You should already have worked out your weak areas and know what is coming – and thus have also worked out what you need to improve. The appraisal isn't a disciplinary interview so any past misdemeanours should have been resolved at the time and not stored up for your appraisal interview. Your appraisal interview is to review progress. That's it. To review how you are doing and apply modifications to make the flow more smooth. The good manager will do this by mutual consent and joint agreement. All you have to do is agree your weak areas. Having them pointed out to you is a blessing, remember that. Don't get defensive, get grateful. Just so long as they construct something new out of it – constructive criticism.

THE MINI APPRAISAL

Just to make sure you have really assessed yourself objectively, ask a friend or colleague to give you a mini appraisal before tomorrow. This can be a very quick thing and need only take about 10 minutes. Just run through your key tasks and say how you think you perform. If they agree move swiftly along. But if they don't you know you have spotlighted a potential problem area. You may say, 'Customer relations, pretty good. Sales techniques, excellent. Following up orders, pretty good.' At the first two they nodded in agreement but at the third one – following up orders – they laugh and say, 'You must be joking, you're bloody hopeless at that, come on.' Now you know which area you need to re-evaluate – and fast.

Your input

Having worked out in advance your own weak points it makes it much slicker to have also worked out the remedies. Then when your boss says, 'And what are we going to do about this?' you'll already have the answer – or at least *an* answer. It may not be the option you go for because your boss will also have worked out a game plan to help you improve on this weak section of your otherwise perfect work performance.

Having worked out in advance your own weak points it makes it much slicker to have also worked out the remedies

So your input is to come up with strategies, suggestions, ideas, discussion points, information, facts, relevant data, support, training programmes, whatever you think is needed to get you back on track. But you must come fully loaded with ideas of some sort (you may not have them ready this time – but next time …). Then when the question comes ('So what are we going to do about this?'), you'll be able to reply, 'Well, I thought a new training module based on the upgrade for the ZX35 would be helpful – I've got some details here. I would also like a bit more back-up in dealing with staff overtime problems – I would welcome your advice about this as I know you've encountered similar problems yourself. I would also request another assistant in the packing areas. That would free up Bill to help me with the customers, which should go a long way to alleviating this particular problem. What do you think, boss?'

Much better than 'Dunno'. And speeds things up as it takes your boss along a route they may already have worked out for themselves and were dreading telling you about in case you got all funny about being retrained on the ZX35 or didn't want to work too closely with Bill or were trying to keep the overtime problem to yourself. Bosses worry a lot about stuff like this, they don't like to step on toes any more than you do. Make it easier for them, make it quicker for them. Seize the initiative, seize the day. In the long run, they'll be impressed with you.

Benefits not features

Current thinking among modern – and slick – advertising executives is that *benefits* is the key word and not *features*. They will say, 'Our new electric sun roof allows you to have the wind in your hair without getting wet,' or some such nonsense rather than, 'Our new sunroof rolls back on titanium bearings and uses new silco runner sealing strips.' And when you ask for additional resources such as training or improvements in your working environment to iron out any weak spots, you too will play up the benefits rather than the features. Why? It's faster. It sells better. It gets across your message slicker and quicker. And that's what fast thinking is all about.

Suppose you need additional training on using the new ZX35. You could present your case by saying, 'This new training programme is designed to be completed in half the usual time, costs about the same as any other and I'll only be out of the office on Monday mornings for twelve weeks.' These are features. Instead say, 'If I was to do this course I could improve the department's output on the ZX35 by some 25 per cent as well as being able to free up some time to get Brenda started on the old ZX34 which I know she's dying to do and I'll have finished it in time to help Tony prepare for the summer exhibition. How's that sound?' Your boss will nod and say it sounds good. They may well then go on to ask about costs and schedules and that sort of thing but they will already have been sold on the idea. If you try to sell 'em features first, they may take the bait or they may not, but if they don't, they won't go on to ask what the benefits might have been. It will already be too late and you have lost your sale – sorry, failed to get your boss to agree additional resources and training. See it as a sales technique and it will be accomplished quicker – fast thinking.

Don't sulk

Suppose your brilliant sales technique fails, what are you going to do? Sulk? Throw a tantrum? No way. If your boss turns you down then turn the tables. Ask them what they see as an ideal way to help you overcome this weak area of yours. If they

BEFORE FLYING OFF THE HANDLE

Before you react to what your boss is saying, make sure you are really sure of your facts. If they say your weak area is in customer relations and you think you are simply brilliant in this department ask them why they think you are not as good as you do. Don't fly off the handle and accuse them of not knowing what they are talking about. They may have some tiny snippet of information that you have overlooked, such as 43 customer complaints about you in the last week alone. Ah.

don't have any solutions you can retry your package. It might work a second time and if it doesn't then you really can't be blamed for failing to improve if your boss isn't helping.

SAUCE FOR THE GANDER

If you give appraisals to junior team members, practise the techniques for good constructive criticisms and make sure you are following the right guidelines – point out the weak area and *jointly* construct a way to improve.

If your boss turns you down then turn the tables. Ask them what they see as an ideal way to help you overcome this weak area of yours

On the other hand your boss may well have suggestions of their own that are completely different from your ideas. Hear them out and see if their ideas might not be better, more cost-effective, faster. Don't jump down their throat. Weigh up the facts before reacting. Discuss their suggestion calmly and reasonably. They will have put some thought into it and may be seeing a bigger picture than you, there may be factors you are unaware of. If there is anything you don't understand then for heaven's sake ask – you won't get another chance until your next appraisal rolls around in six months time.

for next time

Watch your performance as you go along and monitor it so that when your appraisal comes around you will already have lots of ideas about how to improve any weak areas you may have and what sort of training you need.

Make sure you have collected well in advance any brochures or leaflets for training programmes you want.

If there is anything you don't understand then for heaven's sake ask – you won't get another chance until your next appraisal rolls around in six months time

7 action plans and the follow-up

Tomorrow you will go into this appraisal confident, expectant, excitedly anticipating and very secure in your knowledge that you have done everything you need to. Good. But how are you going to come out of it? Relieved? Anxious to put it all behind you and get back to the real work? I do hope not. There's not much more to cover now but what you do after the appraisal might be just as important as – if not more so than – what you do before or during.

JOINT DECISIONS

At the end of your appraisal you will decide jointly on an action plan – that is, what you are *both* going to do to help you improve, advance, progress and generally stay one step ahead of the game.

Remember this is a joint action plan, it must be agreed by both of you. Any manager worth their salt will know that an action plan imposed from on high will simply not work unless they constantly goad you and stand behind you with a whip. Decide it jointly and you will feel much more a part of the process and it will be realistic and feasible, and thus you'll be as anxious to see it through, to see it work, as your boss.

MAKE A NOTE OF THE FOLLOW-UP

This joint action plan may entail your boss going off to find out if you can switch to the packaging department on Thursdays to learn the new procedures, while you enrol on an evening course in A-level bio-physics – you both have something to do. Now the smart and fast thing to do – at the appraisal – is to make some note about how you follow this up: 'So, I'll check with Myra that Thursdays are OK and I'll report back to you by the end of the week at the latest. And you'll let me have details of when you start this course by next Monday, OK?'

This is the follow-up. You should both have, in writing, not only the action plan – what you are going to do – but also what you have to do about what you

What you do after the appraisal might be just as important as – if not more so than – what you do before or during

are going to do – report back, collect more info, research data, confirm, check with someone, liaise with another department – and so on.

Stick to the follow-up

And you must, both of you, stick to the follow-up as much as you stick to the action plan. A breakdown in communications here is not desirable. You must keep each other informed or the process goes to pot. If one of you lets the other down it leads to feelings of not being cared about – that the other wasn't prepared to see things through and is a waste of space and shouldn't be trusted again. You are both probably spending time outside your normal working life investing in each other's future. Your boss collects brownie points as you improve, and you further your experience and skills. It is a mutual thing – you both gain. Don't let each other down in this vital but often overlooked process. The key steps are:

- Jointly decide an action plan.
- Write it down.
- Jointly agree the follow-up.
- Write it down.

- ▶ Follow up.
- ▶ Complete the action plan.
- ▶ Report back at the end of whatever action had to be done.
- ▶ Write this down as well.

REPORTING BACK

It is important that you report back to each other when an action has been completed, or the other will be left wondering. If you do a course, write a short report and give it to your boss outlining:

- ▶ what you learnt
- ▶ how long the course was
- ▶ how effective you considered it to be
- ▶ what benefits you gained from it
- ▶ whether you would recommend it for other team members.

This report needn't be longer than an A4 sheet but it will be useful to your boss. Similarly, when you have finished in the packing department working with Myra on the new procedures you can report back in the same manner.

Your boss collects brownie points as you improve, and you further your experience and skills. It is a mutual thing – you both gain

And then you can be working towards the next appraisal. In the meantime you have your appraisal tomorrow. But you can put you feet up now and enjoy a cup of coffee and a little relaxation, safe in the knowledge that you are ready, prepared, smart and fast. Good luck.

Make sure you have with you details of any courses you have completed since your last appraisal – your boss may want to discuss them in some detail to see how useful they were to you, and could be to other team members.

Check that you have followed up everything that was included in your last appraisal and that you haven't inadvertently overlooked anything – your boss will have a note and it won't look good if you haven't completed a task set you.

You can put you feet up now and enjoy a cup of coffee and a little relaxation, safe in the knowledge that you are ready, prepared, smart and fast

your own appraisal in an hour

You've just looked in your diary and noticed you've got your appraisal in ONE HOUR! What are you going to do? Panic? Not helpful. Take a deep breath and grab a pad and pen. Spend five minutes writing – and thinking about – your objective. Even if you do nothing else, do this. Your objective (see Chapter 1) is: *to have my current work assessed and evaluated with documented feedback, and to have my future work programme reviewed and discussed.*

Let's now work through this logically.

1. Write down the key features of your employment – your key responsibilities.

2. Quickly assess each of these key areas for weaknesses or strengths.

3. Write down what you will need in writing to enable you to improve and progress.

4. Review each key area and decide which ones need work, which ones need further training or whatever it is that will enable you to do them better; and quickly review yourself, of course.

5. Make a note of any points you want to raise concerning the future and how you see your job progressing.

6. You may not have time to collect details of any courses you want to go on but even a quick phone call at this stage is better than nothing – you will have some facts to put before your boss for discussion. The secret is to look prepared even if you're not. If you really had no choice about leaving your appraisal to such a late stage you ought to be using it to look at more effective ways to ease your workload, manage your time and your diary better and somehow stay on top of things.

Spend five minutes writing – and thinking about – your objective. Even if you do nothing else, do this

your own appraisal in 10 minutes

If you really have left it this late you only have one sensible course of action – postponement. Phone your boss now and explain that you need to postpone this appraisal for a day or two. If you are very honest you will explain why. If not invent an excuse but make it good. Good luck.